Junior Drug Awareness
Steroids

Junior Drug Awareness

Alcohol

Amphetamines and Other Uppers

Crack and Cocaine

Ecstasy and Other Designer Drugs

Heroin

How to Get Help

How to Say No

Inhalants and Solvents

LSD, PCP, and Other Hallucinogens

Marijuana

Nicotine and Cigarettes

Pain Relievers, Diet Pills, and
　　Other Over-the-Counter Drugs

Prozac and Other Antidepressants

Steroids

Valium and Other Downers

Junior Drug Awareness

Steroids

Introduction by **BARRY R. McCAFFREY**
Director, Office of National Drug Control Policy

Foreword by **STEVEN L. JAFFE, M.D.**
Senior Consulting Editor,
Professor of Child and Adolescent Psychiatry, Emory University

Dynise Balcavage

Chelsea House Publishers

Philadelphia

CHELSEA HOUSE PUBLISHERS
Editor in Chief Stephen Reginald
Production Manager Pamela Loos
Director of Photography Judy L. Hasday
Art Director Sara Davis
Managing Editor James D. Gallagher
Senior Production Editor LeeAnne Gelletly

Staff for STEROIDS
Project Editor Therese De Angelis
Senior Editor John Ziff
Associate Art Director Takeshi Takahashi
Designer Keith Trego
Picture Researcher Sandy Jones
Cover Illustrator/Designer Takeshi Takahashi

Cover photo © 1997 T&D McCarthy/The Stock Market

The Chelsea House World Wide Web site address is
http://www.chelseahouse.com

 3 5 7 9 8 6 4 2

Library of Congress Cataloging-in-Publication Data

Balcavage, Dynise.
Steroids / Dynise Balcavage : introduction by Barry R.
McCaffrey : foreword by Steven L. Jaffe.
80 pp.   cm. — (Junior drug awareness)
Includes bibliographical references and index.
ISBN 0-7910-5179-X
1. Doping in sports—juvenile literature. 2. Anabolic
steroids—Health aspects—Juvenile literature. I. Title.
II. Series.
RC1230.B35 1999
362.29'9—dc21   99-14077
                                                           CIP
                                                           AC

CONTENTS

Staying Away from Illegal Drugs,   6
Tobacco Products, and Alcohol
Barry R. McCaffrey

Why Should I Learn About Drugs?   10
Steven L. Jaffe, M.D.

1 Athletes in Wonderland   13

2 Body Talk: Steroids   25
and Self-Image

3 The Origin of Anabolic Steroids   33

4 How Steroids Affect the   41
Body and Mind

5 Getting Real: Fighting   57
Steroid Abuse

Glossary   68

Bibliography   73

Find Out More About Steroids,   74
Sports Medicine, and Drug Abuse

You Can't Afford It   77

Index   78

by Barry R. McCaffrey
Director, Office of National
Drug Control Policy

STAYING AWAY FROM ILLEGAL DRUGS, TOBACCO PRODUCTS, AND ALCOHOL

G ood health allows you to be as strong, happy, smart, and skillful as you can possibly be. The worst thing about illegal drugs is that they damage people from the inside. Our bodies and minds are wonderful, complicated systems that run like finely tuned machines when we take care of ourselves.

Doctors prescribe legal drugs, called medicines, to heal us when we become sick, but dangerous chemicals that are not recommended by doctors, nurses, or pharmacists are called illegal drugs. These drugs cannot be bought in stores because they harm different organs of the body, causing illness or even death. Illegal drugs, such as marijuana, cocaine or "crack," heroin, methamphetamine ("meth"), and other dangerous substances are against the law because they affect our ability to think, work, play, sleep, or eat.

If anyone ever offers you illegal drugs or any kind of pills, liquids, substances to smoke, or shots to inject into your body, tell them you're not interested. You should report drug pushers—people who distribute these poisons—to parents, teachers, police, coaches, clergy, or other adults whom you trust.

Cigarettes and alcohol are also illegal for youngsters. Tobacco products and drinks like wine, beer, and liquor are particularly harmful for children and teenagers because their bodies, especially their nervous systems, are still developing. For this reason, young people are more likely to be hurt by illicit drugs—including cigarettes and alcohol. These two products kill more people—from cancer, and automobile accidents caused by intoxicated drivers—than all other drugs combined. We say about drug use: "Users are losers." Be a winner and stay away from illegal drugs, tobacco products, and alcoholic beverages.

Here are four reasons why you shouldn't use illegal drugs:

- Illegal drugs can cause brain damage.
- Illegal drugs are "psychoactive." This means that they change your personality or the way you feel. They also impair your judgment. While under the influence of drugs, you are more likely to endanger your life or someone else's. You will also be less able to protect yourself from danger.
- Many illegal drugs are addictive, which means that once a person starts taking them, stopping is extremely difficult. An addict's body craves the drug and becomes dependent upon it. The illegal drug–user may become sick if the drug is discontinued and so may become a slave to drugs.

- Some drugs, called "gateway" substances, can lead a person to take more-dangerous drugs. For example, a 12-year-old who smokes marijuana is 79 times more likely to have an addiction problem later in life than a child who never tries marijuana.

Here are some reasons why you shouldn't drink alcoholic beverages, including beer and wine coolers:

- Alcohol is the second leading cause of death in our country. More than 100,000 people die every year because of drinking.
- Adolescents are twice as likely as adults to be involved in fatal alcohol-related car crashes.
- Half of all assaults against girls or women involve alcohol.
- Drinking is illegal if you are under the age of 21. You could be arrested for this crime.

Here are three reasons why you shouldn't smoke cigarettes:

- Nicotine is highly addictive. Once you start smoking, it is very hard to stop, and smoking cigarettes causes lung cancer and other diseases. Tobacco- and nicotine-related diseases kill more than 400,000 people every year.
- Each day, 3,000 kids begin smoking. One-third of these youngsters will probably have their lives shortened because of tobacco use.
- Children who smoke cigarettes are almost six times more likely to use other illegal drugs than kids who don't smoke.

If your parents haven't told you how they feel about the dangers of illegal drugs, ask them. One of every 10 kids aged 12 to 17 is using illegal drugs. They do not understand the risks they are taking with their health and their lives. However, the vast majority of young people in America are smart enough to figure out that drugs, cigarettes, and alcohol could rob them of their future. Be your body's best friend: guard your mental and physical health by staying away from drugs.

WHY SHOULD I LEARN ABOUT DRUGS?

Steven L. Jaffe, M.D., Senior Consulting Editor,
Professor of Child and Adolescent Psychiatry,
Emory University

Your grandparents and great-grandparents did not think much about "drug awareness." That's because drugs, to most of them, simply meant "medicine."

Of the three types of drugs, medicine is the good type. Medicines such as penicillin and aspirin promote healing and help sick people get better.

Another type of drug is obviously bad for you because it is poison. Then there are the kinds of drugs that fool you, such as marijuana and LSD. They make you feel good, but they harm your body and brain.

Our great crisis today is that this third category of drugs has become widely abused. Drugs of abuse are everywhere, not just in rough neighborhoods. Many teens are introduced to drugs by older brothers, sisters, friends, or even friends' parents. Some people may use only a little bit of a drug, but others who inherited a tendency to become addicted may move on to using drugs all the time. If a family member is or was an alcoholic or an addict, a young person is at greater risk of becoming one.

Drug abuse can weaken us physically. Worse, it can cause permanent mental damage. Our brain is the most important part of our body. Our thoughts, hopes, wishes, feelings, and memories are located there, within 100 billion nerve cells. Alcohol and drugs that are abused will harm—and even destroy—these cells. During the teen years, your brain continues to develop and grow, but drugs and alcohol can impair this growth.

I treat all types of teenagers at my hospital programs and in my office. Many suffer from depression or anxiety. A lot of them abuse drugs and alcohol, and this makes their depression or fears worse. I have celebrated birthdays and high school graduations with many of my patients. But I have also been to sad funerals for others who have died from problems with drug abuse.

Doctors understand more about drugs today than ever before. We've learned that some substances (even some foods) that we once thought were harmless can actually cause health problems. And for some people, medicines that help relieve one symptom might cause problems in other ways. This is because each person's body chemistry and immune system are different.

For all of these reasons, drug awareness is important for everyone. We need to learn which drugs to avoid or question—not only the destructive, illegal drugs we hear so much about in the news, but also ordinary medicines we buy at the supermarket or pharmacy. We need to understand that even "good" drugs can hurt us if they are not used correctly. We also need accurate scientific knowledge, not just rumors we hear from other teens.

Drug awareness enables you to make good decisions. It allows you to become powerful and strong and have a meaningful life!

Despite what you may hear, using steroids or other performance-enhancing drugs does not guarantee athletic success. Read this book to find out how steroid abuse can damage your health.

1

ATHLETES IN WONDERLAND

I n the famous children's book *Alice's Adventures in Wonderland* by Lewis Carroll, Alice, the main character, lives in a world where virtually anything can happen. When Alice first descends into the rabbit hole, she spies a little glass box lying under a table. She opens it, and in it finds a tiny cake, on which the words "eat me" are beautifully marked in currants. "Well, I'll eat it," Alice decides,

and if it makes me grow larger, I can reach the key; and if it makes me grow smaller, I can creep under the door; so either way I'll get into the garden, and I don't care which happens!

She ate a little bit and said anxiously to herself, "Which way? Which way?" holding her hand on the top of her head to feel which way it was growing, and

was quite surprised to find that she remained the same size: to be sure, this generally happens when one eats cake, but Alice had got so much into the way of expecting nothing but out-of-the-way things to happen, that it seemed quite dull and stupid for life to go on in the common way.

Alice's Adventures in Wonderland is filled with fantastic images. Alice encounters amazing creatures and takes incredible journeys. Unfortunately, like this make-believe character, some athletes are unable to distinguish fantasy from reality.

Real life also has its share of amazing characters and incredible journeys, but it also has real consequences that depend upon the choices you make. There are good and bad sides to any choice you make in life. Some athletes who have chosen to abuse steroids, however, have done so without fully understanding the consequences of their choices—for themselves as well as their families and friends.

In the 1970s, Lyle Alzado was an extremely successful professional football player. After he retired, Alzado developed brain cancer. Formerly a strong and aggressive All-Pro defensive end who played for the Denver Broncos and Cleveland Browns, as well as the Oakland Raiders (1971–85), Alzado blamed his disease on the steroids he had abused for almost 20 years.

"It was addicting, mentally addicting," Alzado said of the drugs that he believed contributed to the cancer that eventually took his life in 1991 at age 43. "I just

Because anabolic (or "building") steroids mimic the muscle-building effects of the male sex hormone testosterone, they are often used by body-builders who want to increase muscle mass.

didn't feel strong unless I was taking something. When I retired, I kept taking the stuff. I couldn't stand the thought of being weak."

Ironically, the steroids that enlarged Alzado's muscles and made him feel strong may have ultimately weakened him to such a degree that he could not get out of bed. He developed brain lymphoma, a form of cancer that killed him 13 months after he was diagnosed. At the time of his death, Alzado barely possessed the strength of a two-year-old. "I know there's no written, documented proof that steroids and human growth hormone caused this cancer," Alzado said before he died. "But it's one of the reasons you have to look at. You have to."

"All the NFL has to do to keep players from using

steroids is to include the 'Lyle Alzado story' in every player's playbook," says Thomas "Hollywood" Henderson, a former Dallas Cowboys linebacker. If only the solution were so simple. In reality, athletes seem to have taken little warning from the life and death of Lyle Alzado. As you will discover in the following chapters, steroid abuse is a complicated problem with many possible causes—feelings of low self-worth, an overemphasis on winning at all costs, and obsessive concern about body image, to name a few. Unfortunately, complicated problems do not have easy solutions.

Athletes at Risk

If you wanted to sell a lot of lollipops, chances are that you would set up your candy stand in front of a playground rather than a dentist's office. The people who illegally sell steroids and other **performance-enhancing drugs**, also known as **ergogenic drugs**, also know how to "target" their customers. Steroids are aimed at athletes, many of whom want bigger muscles at any cost. Slick advertisements promising to build muscles and enhance athletic performance are frequently found in bodybuilding and sports magazines or around gyms. Unfortunately, these ads often neglect to point out how much athletes stand to lose by taking steroids—their health and their lives, for example.

Bigger, Stronger, Faster

Anabolic steroid abuse is usually associated with sports, from grade school to professional levels.

Although most high school and elementary school sports coaches stress the importance of good health habits and nutrition, a few have pressured their athletes to take steroids to make them run faster, grow stronger, and perform better.

Despite the fact that steroids have been abused for years, especially in professional team sports and body-building, the news media began reporting the problem only after several athletes tested positive for the drug. Perhaps the best-known steroid user is Canadian sprinter Ben Johnson. Johnson was stripped of the gold medal he won at the 1988 Olympics in Seoul, South Korea, after a drug test he took came up positive for the presence of steroids. Because of Johnson's drug use, his world-record time of 9.79 seconds in the 100-meter race was declared invalid. In 1993, he again tested positive for steroid use and was banned for life from world competition.

Johnson's story brought international attention to the problem of steroid abuse. Many people questioned whether it was fair for an athlete who was propped up with drugs to compete against drug-free athletes. More recently, the entire cycling team from France was expelled from the 1998 Tour de France bicycle race for using performance-enhancing drugs.

A Team Effort

Fortunately, most doctors put the health of their patients first. But more and more sports team doctors are feeling pressure to prescribe steroids. (Most professional sports organizations have a team physician as

Think that using steroids will bring you fame? At the finish line of the 100-meter men's track and field event in the 1988 Summer Olympics, Canadian star Ben Johnson (far left) glances at his main rival, American runner Carl Lewis (far right). Johnson was stripped of the gold medal he received in this race after he tested positive for steroids.

well as team trainers.) And unfortunately, some actually condone (approve of) using harmful drugs to boost athletic performance.

Dr. Robert Kerr, author of a book about steroids, displays some of the faulty logic that leads some athletes to try steroids. He compares steroids to inventions that help make athletes perform better, such as improved running shoes, faster tracks, and more flexible pole-vaulting poles. "After all," he writes, "this new technology was developed to give greater gains with less effort—isn't that why anabolics [steroids] are taken?"

It can be hard to say no to steroids when some medical doctors condone their use or even prescribe them. Athletes might feel intimidated by a physician's expertise, or they may just take for granted that a trained medical professional knows best. Sometimes, they may not even be aware that a substance a doctor has prescribed is actually a steroid.

But more and more doctors who prescribe steroids to children and teens are being held responsible for their actions. In 1998, after former East German sports doctor Dieter Binus admitted prescribing steroids, he and four other doctors were charged with causing bodily harm to 19 swimmers—who were teenagers at the time—by giving them anabolic steroids without informing them or their parents.

"All Natural"?

Even readily available "all-natural" supplements are not always as healthful as they might seem. In 1998, teenage tennis star Samantha Reeves opted to boost her performance by taking a dietary supplement advertised as natural. The product, widely available over the counter in many health food stores, was supposed to help her burn fat and build muscle.

Unfortunately, Reeves's decision to use this supplement was not a good one. Much to her shock, Reeves failed a **urine test** that detects improper drug use and is required of all tennis players. (Because residue from drugs or other substances can be detected in the urine,

athletes undergoing drug testing must submit a sample of their urine. The sample is then analyzed in a laboratory to determine whether the athlete has used drugs of any kind.) Reeves found out that the supplement she was taking contained a substance called Nor-Andro 19, a variation of the well-known steroid **nandrolone**, which is banned by professional tennis. Although Reeves apparently did not intend to take any illegal drugs, she earned the unfortunate distinction of being the first female tennis player ever to test positive for steroids.

Many experts believe that Reeves truly was unaware of the ingredients in the supplement she was taking. Alan Jones is a professor of **pharmaceuticals** (medicinal drugs) at the University of Mississippi. He also acts as the **toxicology** consultant to the company that administers drug testing for the International Tennis Federation. "It's conceivable that a player could be oblivious to the fact that they're using something that contains an anabolic substance," says Jones. "They think: It's natural, it's pure, it's good for me. And that is an absolute [lie]."

How Safe Are the Alternatives?

So-called steroid "alternatives," like the one Samantha Reeves took, are also targeted at athletes. Two steroid alternatives commonly used by athletes are **gamma hydroxybutyrate (GHB)** and **clenbuterol**. Advertisers of these substances claim that these compounds are natural and produce no side effects. GHB is even believed to be a neurotransmitter (brain chemical) in the human body.

Former NFL offensive lineman Steve Courson at home in Farmington, PA, in 1997. After he was cut by Tampa Bay when he admitted he had used steroids, Courson sued the NFL, claiming that the organization failed to enforce its anti-drug policy. He also claimed that his present heart condition is the result of steroid abuse during his nine-year career with the NFL.

But are they safe to take as supplements? It is important to consider the effects of these products on your body. If you are an athlete—or even if you want to look better or perform better athletically—you might think that taking a product like GHB is a good alternative to taking steroids. But before you do this, ask yourself this question: how natural is it to take a substance that forces your muscles to grow faster than normal?

Compounds such as GHB and clenbuterol have dangerous side effects. GHB can cause headaches, nausea, vomiting, diarrhea, seizures, and other central nervous system disorders—and it can kill you. Unfortunately, as a September 30, 1996, article in *Time* magazine reported, GHB has also become popular in recent years as a "social" drug, used to produce relaxation and mild euphoria during parties and "raves" (all-night dance parties). Odorless and colorless with a slightly salty taste, GHB is not only illegal but also extremely dangerous. Just one use can cause coma or death. In Texas in 1996, a 17-year-old star athlete and good student went to a dance party where she drank a few soft drinks. That night, she complained of a headache and nausea. The following day, she was dead from an overdose of GHB, which experts believe may have been slipped into her drinks.

Clenbuterol has become an extremely popular item on the **black market** (the business of selling, buying, or distributing illegal goods). The drug is used in some countries to treat sick animals but is not approved for human use in the United States. One recent news report about clenbuterol was especially frightening: in Spain, 135 people became ill with muscle tremors, rapid heart rates, headaches, dizziness, nausea, fever, and chills after eating beef liver that contained residues of the drug.

A Necessary Evil?

Does an athlete really need steroids to perform well? In 1990, weightlifting and bodybuilding champion Richard L. Sandlin, who had also been an assistant football coach at the University of Alabama, testified before the U.S. House of Representatives Subcommittee on Crime. Sandlin described his experience as a steroid abuser:

> I took steroids from 1976 to 1983. In the middle of 1979, my body began turning a yellowish color. I was very aggressive and combative, had high blood pressure and testicular atrophy [shrunken testicles]. I was hospitalized twice with near-kidney failure, liver tumors and severe personality disorders. During my second hospital stay, the doctors found that I had become sterile [unable to father a child].
>
> Two years after I quit using [steroids] and started training without drugs, I set six new world records in power lifting, something I thought was impossible without the steroids.

Today, Sandlin heads Sandco Sports Nutrition, an organization dedicated to teaching schools, universities, and professional sports teams how to run successful, drug-free training programs.

As Sandlin's story shows, it *is* possible to be athletically competitive without abusing steroids. Moreover, you're far more likely to have a healthy future in sports without these drugs. In the next chapter, we'll explore the many reasons why kids—and even grownups—try steroids in the first place.

There's nothing wrong with wanting to get in shape or build muscle tone. However, those who try the "quick fix" of using steroids not only endanger their health, but they may also find themselves weaker and smaller in the long run.

2

BODY TALK: STEROIDS AND SELF-IMAGE

E very day, on TV, in magazines, and in movies, we are bombarded with images of slim, well-toned models and athletes. They appear to be healthy, happy, and well adjusted. Not surprisingly, we admire them and want to be like them.

Unfortunately, most of us can't look and feel so wonderful all the time. The idealized images we see in the media can lead us to believe that our own bodies are too ugly, too skinny, or too fat in comparison. But the fact is, no one's body is perfect. Even models and athletes have flaws.

Right or wrong, people in the United States—even young children—feel pressure to achieve impossibly perfect bodies. To attain what they consider an ideal figure, some people will go to extremes, such as dieting excessively, taking steroids or diet pills, undergoing plastic

One of the most noticeable side effects of steroid abuse is increased aggressiveness and irritability—a syndrome described by athletes as "'roid rage."

surgery, or even becoming bulimic (bingeing on food and then vomiting afterward to avoid gaining weight). Since most of us view athletes and slim celebrities as role models, it can be difficult to understand that having a perfect body does not make one's life perfect.

Just for Boys

The fact that women and girls have long been preoccupied with their bodies is well documented. But most people do not realize that many boys and men are also unhappy with their bodies. Unfortunately, just as girls may turn to unhealthy practices to gain a better figure, dissatisfaction with one's appearance can lead boys to engage in excessive exercise and steroid abuse.

Steroid abuse often begins in high school. Girls in their early teens undergo a growth spurt that most boys will not experience until they are about two years older. During this period, many boys are shorter than their female classmates. Although this is quite normal, boys of this age often feel that they are too small or too thin, and that they need to gain weight to look strong or attractive. Negative feelings about their bodies tempt many boys to try steroids. All too often, they end up addicted.

Dr. Ronald Harris, a **pathologist** (a doctor who studies the causes and nature of disease), estimates that almost 400,000 adolescents have used steroids to inhance their athletic performance. "They're thinking 'I want to be the best runner,'" he says. "'I want to be the best weight lifter. I want to be the best wrestler and I want to get there at all costs.'"

How does steroid abuse begin? While women and girls often see themselves as heavier than they really are, studies have shown that many men see themselves as smaller and thinner than they really are. And just as girls sometimes disregard health risks and go on extreme diets to lose weight, more high school and college males are taking steroids to bulk up and develop muscular physiques. The seemingly positive effects of taking steroids—bigger muscles and better athletic perfor-mance—can appear quickly. They can be so rewarding that a boy can easily become addicted before he under-stands the harmful **side effects** of steroid abuse.

'Roid Rage

Steroids can have an ugly psychological effect on people who abuse them. One of the most common symptoms of steroid abuse is increased aggression, hostility, or destructive behavior. Although the abuser may not notice any changes in his or her personality, they are usually apparent to friends and family. The steroid abuser might seem unusually irritable or short-tempered. Things that would not normally disturb most people might send a steroid abuser into a rage or a tantrum. This behavior is known in athletic circles as **'roid rage**.

This level of aggression is not acceptable in school or in most social situations, but it is sometimes encouraged in athletic contexts, where some coaches view it as "competitive." If you were a football coach, for instance, who would you choose to play on your team: a nice, even-tempered guy, or an aggressive, raging athlete?

After years of steroid abuse, athletes will almost always suffer some long-term effects. But these consequences often show up years later. The hazards of steroids are like icebergs: you can see only the tip of them looming above the surface, but underneath they can be deadly.

Girls Are Not Immune

Males are not the only ones who use steroids. More and more women have been turning to these drugs to improve their athletic performance and appearance. In the 1980 Olympics, two athletes from each sports team

Do your friends look like this? Probably not! No one has a "perfect" body. Even well-toned athletes, bodybuilders, and models have physical imperfections.

were picked randomly and tested for drugs. Several women—including Bulgarian world-class runner Totka Petrova; Romanian Natalia Maracescu, who held the world mile record for women; and Romanian Ileana Silai, a 1968 silver medalist in the 800-meter track and field event—were banned for life from international competition when they tested positive for performance-enhancing drugs.

When ingested over a long period of time, steroids give females a masculine appearance, characterized by overdeveloped muscles and a low percentage of body fat. (Women's bodies naturally have a higher percentage of fat than men's bodies.) Women may also develop deeper voices and more body hair. And steroid use is just as risky for girls as it is for boys. Read Chapter 4 for more information about what steroids can do to your body and mind.

Steroids and the Internet

As the Internet becomes increasingly popular, information about how to purchase and use steroids becomes readily available at the click of a mouse. Unfortunately, there is no way to regulate this information to protect those who read or use it. Much of what is published on the Internet is inaccurate, incomplete, or even worse, just plain wrong.

One site on steroids, for example, explains in great detail how to exercise and take steroids to bulk up, but does not contain any information about the harmful side effects of steroids. Some of the steroid compounds hawked on the Internet may even be illegal!

What does this mean? Don't believe everything you read. Those who advertise steroids, even if they are adults, do not have your best interests at heart.

The Key to Unlocking Other Problems

Abuse of any drug is a sign that even bigger problems exist in the user's life. If everyone felt comfortable with his or her body, for example, no one would be anorexic, have plastic surgery, or take steroids. Unfortunately, many drug problems stem from feelings of powerlessness in other areas of life.

Steroid abusers might feel that family problems or difficulties in school are out of their control. Taking steroids and bulking up becomes something that abusers can control, and this can make them feel powerful, not only physically but also emotionally. What most users don't realize is that without steroids, they are neither helpless nor powerless. In the next chapter, we'll learn how this source of false strength and power became widely available for abuse.

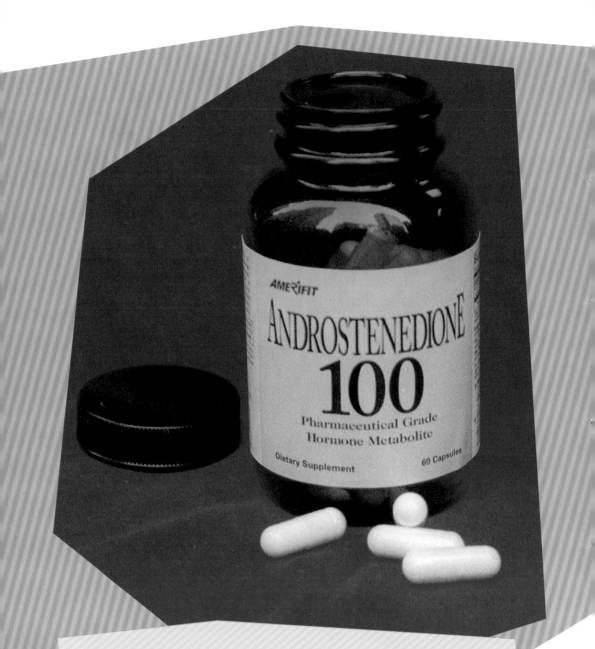

This "dietary supplement" may look harmless, but it is actually a steroid. Although it is banned by the NFL and the International Olympic Committee, it is still legal in the United States. The use of steroids among professional athletes is not new: beginning in the 1950s, athletes in Europe began using the drugs as performance enhancers.

THE ORIGIN OF ANABOLIC STEROIDS

The drive to compete athletically—and to win—is as old as humankind itself. Athletes throughout history have sought ways to increase their strength and performance by taking special foods and other substances into their bodies. In ancient Greece, wrestlers ate huge quantities of meat to build muscle. Norse warriors ingested hallucinogenic (mind-altering) plants to prepare themselves for battle.

The first known athletes to practice **doping** (using non-food substances to improve their performance) were Dutch swimmers in the 1860s. Since then, other athletes have used substances like strychnine (a poison), caffeine, cocaine, and heroin in an attempt to get an edge on the competition.

In the late 1800s, scientists confirmed the effects of

Most U.S. cattle raised for beef are fed government-approved hormones and antibiotics to make them grow faster and to ward off infection and disease. Some people, however, are concerned about consuming these substances in their food, and eat only beef products derived from "free-range" cattle, which are allowed to range and forage with few restrictions.

male steroid **hormones**, which they called **androgens**, by performing experiments on roosters. They castrated the roosters (removed their testicles) and discovered that the birds could still maintain a normal comb and wattle (the fleshy appendages on a male chicken's head and under its beak) if they were given **testosterone**. Testosterone is the main androgen produced by the testicles in humans and animals.

By the 1930s, steroids were isolated and used to treat anemia (a condition in which the blood does not have enough iron) and other diseases that cause muscles to waste or grow smaller. Doctors also used steroids to treat patients with cancer, burns, intestinal problems, and asthma.

More intensive research on testosterone began in the 1940s and 1950s. Doctors realized that the **anabolic**, or tissue-building, properties of testosterone could be helpful in treating some illnesses and injuries. Even this early in their research, physicians tried to find ways to minimize the **androgenic** (masculinizing) effects that steroids had on patients.

The first "athlete" to have his performance enhanced by testosterone was actually a racehorse named Halloway. Before he was implanted with testosterone pellets, the 18-year-old gelding had grown slow and seemed less willing to race; his endurance level had also dropped. After several months of training, combined with the testosterone implants, Halloway performed well in several races and even set a trotting record.

Steroids and Athletes

European athletes began experimenting with steroids as performance enhancers in the early 1950s. They discovered that steroids did indeed improve certain aspects of their athletic performance. Their bodies became leaner, their muscles became bigger and stronger, and they became more aggressive. At the 1952 Summer Olympics in Helsinki, Finland, the Soviet weight lifting team took several medals, thanks in part to steroid use. Word spread quickly in athletic circles, and a new trend began— ingesting steroids to boost athletic performance. Dr. Tom

Waddell, a former decathlete, estimated that about one-third of the 1968 U.S. Olympic track and field team used steroids while preparing for the Games. Steroids had become an undeniable presence in American athletics.

Around the same time, steroids became extremely popular among professional football players. Former Dallas Cowboys offensive lineman Pat Donovan said, "Anabolic steroids are very, very accepted in the NFL. In the last five or six years, [their use] ran as high as 60 to 70 percent [among] the Cowboys." Many other professional football players, including Fred Smerlas of the Buffalo Bills and Joe Klecko of the New York Jets, have offered similar estimates.

Today, more than 100 synthetic anabolic steroids exist. All of them have dangerous side effects if taken in large enough doses. For example, **erythropoietin (EPO)** is a genetic copy of a hormone that stimulates the production of oxygen-rich red blood cells. Although it effectively treats kidney disease, anemia, and other disorders, EPO is also popular among long-distance runners, cross-country skiers, and distance swimmers who want to increase their endurance. Thus far, EPO has been blamed for 24 deaths among competitive cyclists. The synthetic hormone thickens the blood, which may increase the risk of heart attacks in people who use it.

Steroids and the Law

In 1975, the use of steroids by Olympic athletes was banned by the International Olympic Committee, which began requiring urine tests for all athletes competing in the Games. Since then, most major amateur and professional sports organizations have also included anabolic steroids on their lists of banned substances. These groups include the NFL, the National Collegiate Athletic Association, the International Amateur Athletic Federation, and the International Federation of Body Builders.

In 1988, the U.S. Congress passed the Anti-Drug Abuse Act, which made distributing or possessing anabolic steroids for nonmedical reasons a federal offense. An even newer law, the Anabolic Steroids Act of 1990, recategorized anabolic steroids as controlled substances and increased penalties for steroid use and trafficking. The 1990 act also imposed strict regulations on pharmaceutical firms who manufacture the drug for medical purposes. To date, more than 25 states have passed their own laws combating steroid abuse, and others are considering similar laws.

Fortunately, many of the laws include steroid substitutes that can be just as harmful to athletes as steroids themselves. At the 1992 Summer Olympics in Barcelona, Spain, athletes from several countries, including Germany, the United States, China, Great Britain, and the former Soviet Union, were not allowed to compete because of evidence that they had used nonsteroid drugs meant to mimic the effects of steroids.

Where Do Steroids Come From?

Today, most anabolic steroids come from one of three sources. Some are made legally or illegally outside the United States and smuggled into this country, often

through the mail. Some are made legally in this country by pharmaceutical companies for medical use, but are then acquired by distributors on the black market. Others are created in secret, illegal laboratories in the United States. These steroids are perhaps the most dangerous variety because they are not subject to the strict regulations that guarantee the purity and strength of medically approved substances. The U.S. Customs Service (the bureau that regulates items brought into the United States from other countries) has seized illegal steroids from many countries, including Italy, Portugal, France, Mexico, Great Britain, Brazil, and Peru.

Athletes Speak Out Against Steroids

Some athletes who once abused steroids themselves have begun to speak out against their use. They are giving young people testimony about the way these drugs have harmed their bodies.

Former NFL offensive lineman Steve Courson, for example, is now living with a debilitating heart condition, which he blames on steroid abuse during his nine-year career (1977–85). During this period, Courson took about 56 ounces of performance-enhancing drugs each week, and he gained as many as 30 pounds in a single month. In 1985, after revealing his steroid abuse to the public, Courson was cut by Tampa Bay. Clearly, athletes are sometimes still expected to play the steroid game without telling—or forsake their careers if they speak out.

In the 1990s, steroid use became more popular

A U.S. Drug Enforcement Agency official (left) and a U.S. customs officer hold a news conference near a Russian cargo ship at a Pennsylvania marine terminal in 1995. A former Russian hockey player was arrested for arranging to transport $650,000 worth of steroids into the United States. Such commerce became illegal in 1988 with the Anti-Drug Abuse Act.

among adolescents. Studies show that 6 to 10 percent of high school boys and one percent of high school girls will use steroids before they graduate. Two-thirds of this group will use them before they are 16 years old. Most young adults take steroids to improve their performance as athletes. But as many as 25 percent of adolescents surveyed take steroids simply to improve their appearance.

These percentages might be lower if more kids learn exactly what anabolic steroids can do to your mind and body. In the next chapter, we'll examine some of the dangerous effects of steroid use.

Who needs steroids? Read Chapters 4 and 5 to find out what these drugs do to you and why you don't need them to stay strong and healthy.

4

HOW STEROIDS AFFECT THE BODY AND MIND

Steroids are powerful drugs that can both heal and harm. But exactly what are they? In order to find out, we need to learn not only about the brain, but also about the human body's **endocrine system**, which is responsible for producing and regulating hormones.

Steroids and Your Brain

The parts of your brain that influence your moods and are involved in learning and memory are called the **limbic system**. Anabolic steroids act in this area. In animals, anabolic steroids have been shown to impair learning and memory. They can also be responsible for changes in mood, such as feelings of depression and irritability. Anabolic steroid users may act unkindly toward people they're normally nice to, such as friends and

family. They may also develop 'roid rage—exceptionally aggressive behavior.

Whether you are male or female, your body's testosterone production is controlled by a group of nerve cells at the base of the brain called the **hypothalamus**. This part of the brain also controls appetite, blood pressure, and moods. Anabolic steroids change the messages that the hypothalamus sends to the body, disrupting normal hormone function.

The Endocrine System

The body's endocrine system controls its internal hormone **secretions**. Picture your body as a large farm and the endocrine system as a sprinkler system. To function normally, a part of the body needs to be "sprinkled" with a hormone created by a related endocrine **gland** (such as the **adrenal glands** or the **testes**). The hormones are released directly into the bloodstream or **lymph** (clear fluid containing white blood cells). Each of the endocrine glands has a specific function.

Generally speaking, hormones regulate cellular activity. As adolescents approach adulthood, for example, their pituitary gland secretes many hormones. These hormones cause boys and girls to grow into men and women. Hormones are continually secreted, produced, made inactive, and eliminated. The secretion rates of each hormone change depending on the body's needs.

Men and women secrete the same kinds of hormones, but in different amounts. Men primarily secrete testosterone and androgen, while women secrete mostly

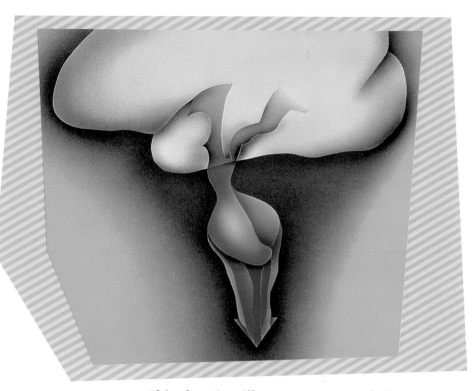

This drawing illustrates some of the regions of the brain that are affected by steroids. The area between the two green bands is the hypothalamus, which controls appetite, blood pressure, moods, and testosterone production. The hypothalamus stimulates the pituitary gland (shown in blue) to produce a growth hormone, which is released into the bloodstream.

estrogen and **progesterone**. In adult males, testosterone is produced mainly in the testes. In women and girls, low levels of testosterone are produced in the **ovaries** and the adrenal glands.

What Anabolic Steroids Do to You

Anabolic steroids are artificial or natural compounds made to act like testosterone. Human testosterone causes

many of the sex characteristics that young boys develop at **puberty**, such as the enlargement of the sex organs and the growth of facial and body hair. Testosterone also stimulates some growth and development of blood, muscle, and bone.

When steroids change the messages that the brain sends to the body via hormones, they also cause changes in the body. In boys, steroids interfere with the normal production of testosterone. They also act directly on the testes and cause them to shrink. This can result in a lower sperm count and affect a person's ability to father children. Steroids can also cause irreversible hair loss.

In girls, anabolic steroids can cause the menstrual period to stop by acting on both the hypothalamus and the reproductive organs. They can also cause hair loss from the head, growth of body and facial hair, and deepening of the voice. These changes are also irreversible.

Dependence and Addiction

People who abuse anabolic steroids pay a high price, both literally and figuratively, for a bit of muscle growth. Since the so-called "benefits" of taking steroids can be immediate and pronounced, users may begin to feel as though they need to take the drugs to feel normal or to perform at a consistently high level. A runner, for example, might believe that he cannot race well without taking steroids. And since abusers may lose weight after quitting steroids, they may fear getting small or weak, which makes quitting even more difficult. This makes some users feel tempted to take steroids again to gain back the

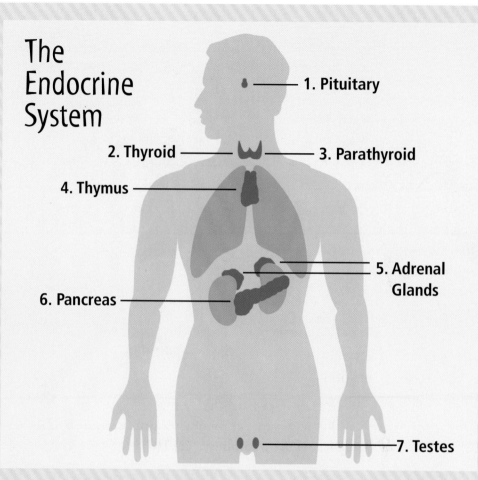

The Endocrine System

1. Pituitary

2. Thyroid — 3. Parathyroid

4. Thymus

5. Adrenal Glands

6. Pancreas

7. Testes

This drawing shows the different glands that make up the human endocrine system: 1) the pituitary, which is in the brain, 2) the thyroid and 3) parathyroid, which are situated in front of the larynx (or voice box), 4) the thymus, which is located near the heart, 5) the adrenal glands, which sit on top of each kidney, 6) the pancreas, located near the kidneys, and 7) sex glands, which are the testes in males (shown here) and the ovaries in females. Steroids work by disrupting the normal functions of the endocrine system: in boys, they interfere with testosterone production and cause testicles to shrink; in girls, they affect the reproductive organs, causing a deepening voice and hair growth on the body and face.

This diagram shows how blood circulates from the heart and lungs to the rest of the body. Arteries (shown in red) carry oxygen-rich blood to the body from the heart; veins (shown in blue) return oxygen-depleted blood to the heart, where it is once again oxygenated by the lungs. Steroids can cause a chemical imbalance that disrupts this process and leads to hypertension (high blood pressure).

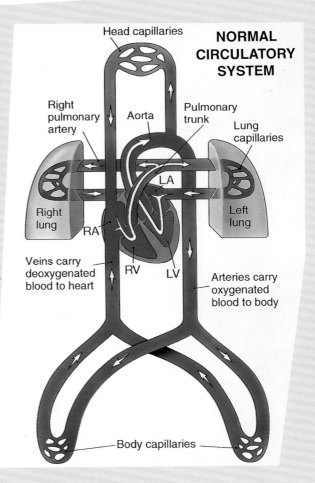

Head capillaries

NORMAL CIRCULATORY SYSTEM

Right pulmonary artery

Aorta

Pulmonary trunk

Lung capillaries

LA

Right lung

RA

Left lung

Veins carry deoxygenated blood to heart

RV

LV

Arteries carry oxygenated blood to body

Body capillaries

weight they lost. When this occurs, the abuser has developed a **psychological dependence** on the drugs.

Some recent studies suggest that taking megadoses of anabolic steroids may lead to **addiction**, or **physical dependence**. This means that a person's body has changed to adapt to the abused drug and cannot function normally without it. Researchers at Yale University have found that long-term steroid users experience many of the characteristics of addiction, including cravings for the drug, difficulty in quitting, and **withdrawal** symptoms, which occur when people who are addicted to a drug try to stop taking it.

The symptoms of withdrawal vary depending on the drug that is abused. Steroid abusers undergoing withdrawal may experience depression, insomnia (inability to sleep), appetite loss, or weakness. They may also suffer from headaches, nausea, or excessive sweating. Sometimes, a steroid abuser experiences increased anxiety—a feeling of uneasiness and distress—that can lead to disturbed sleep patterns or sleepwalking.

Growing Bigger, Staying Smaller

Young people can suffer one of the gravest effects of steroid abuse. Steroids can trick the body into thinking that it is producing enough testosterone. When it senses that it has enough, it shuts down any functions involving this hormone. For example, the body begins to fuse the long bones of the body and make them stop growing during late adolescence. Steroids can artificially speed up this process: in the end, a child's growth can stop prematurely. For this reason, a young adult who takes steroids to get bigger may actually end up not reaching his or her full potential height.

Steroids and Your Liver

The liver, one of body's most important organs, is also severely affected by steroid use. The liver removes impurities from the body, acting like a filter in a pool that keeps the water safe for swimming. The liver produces **bile**, a pigment that comes from bodily waste

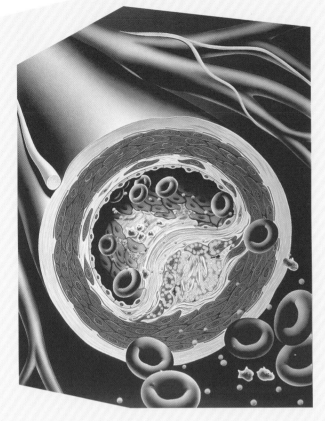

This drawing, a cross-section of a human artery, shows what can happen when steroids are abused over long periods of time. When fatty deposits (shown in yellow) begin to build up within the walls of the artery, they partially block the flow of blood through the vessel. As a result, the heart has to work harder to move the blood through the body. This dangerous condition is known as atherosclerosis.

products. Steroid users' bile production can rise to dangerous levels. The drugs can also interrupt the flow of bile, causing a serious condition called intrahepatic cholestasis. Steroids have also been associated with **gallstones**—small, hard deposits of minerals in the gallbladder or bile ducts that can be extremely painful.

One of the most serious consequences of steroid abuse is a condition in which blood-filled cysts form in the liver. When these cysts burst, they can cause liver failure, which can be fatal. Luckily, some evidence shows that once a person stops taking anabolic steroids, these cysts will shrink or even disappear. Anabolic steroids have also been associated with cancer of the liver. The cancer may be curable once the patient stops taking steroids.

Steroid abuse may also be a factor in other forms of cancer. When a person's ratio of male to female hormones is disturbed, the imbalance of hormones can cause cells to mutate or become irregular and can cause changes to the metabolic system, possibly resulting in cancer. The average adult male naturally produces 2.5 to 11 milligrams of testosterone daily. The average steroid abuser might ingest more than 100 milligrams a day!

Other side effects of steroid abuse include increased appetite, energy, and tolerance to pain. Many steroid users experience nightmares or disturbed sleep. Some become depressed and lethargic (sluggish) when they try to quit using the drugs.

Steroids and Your Heart

One of the worst effects of steroid abuse is heart disorders. The heart keeps us alive by pumping oxygen-rich blood throughout our bodies via about 60,000 miles of blood vessels. Steroid abuse can damage this vital organ in several ways. The user can develop **hypertension** (high blood pressure): steroids elevate the amount of nitrogen the body stores, causing the body to compensate for the chemical imbalance by retaining more water. The retained fluid creates a condition called **edema**, which can elevate the body's blood pressure and make the heart work harder than it should. This sometimes results in heart failure.

Steroids can also cause a disease known as **athero-sclerosis**, in which the **arteries** (blood vessels that carry blood from the heart to the body) become blocked by fatty substances. The disease almost killed nine-time world powerlifting champion and steroid user Larry Pacifico when he was only 35 years old. "One day in the fall of 1981, I was in the recovery room of a hospital following elbow surgery," Pacifico recalled in a 1983 interview with *Sports Illustrated* magazine, "and I had this terrible squeezing in my chest. . . . The next morning . . . I learned that two of my arteries were approximately 70 percent blocked and one was almost closed completely."

After emergency surgery, Pacifico recovered. "I'm convinced my steroid use contributed to my coronary artery disease," he said. "I should have realized it was happening because every time I went on a cycle of heavy steroid use I'd develop high blood pressure and my pulse rate would increase."

An Expensive Habit

Steroids are usually taken orally (by mouth) or by injection. Athletes and other people who abuse these drugs take them daily for weeks or months at a time, in patterns called **cycling**. A person who is cycling takes steroids over a certain period of time (12 weeks, for example), stops for a period of time (perhaps 6 weeks), and then begins the schedule again. Abusers often take 20 to 200 times the daily dose that a doctor would prescribe for an ailment. Some abusers also practice **stacking**—combining several different brands of steroids to

These women are competing in a New Hampshire body-building competition. Most of what you hear about steroid abuse involves boys and men, but the problem is also growing among girls and women, who are increasingly becoming involved in pro sports and bodybuilding.

increase their results and limit their side effects. A single cycle can cost thousands of dollars: serious abusers may spend more than $400 per week on anabolic steroids, and professional athletes who abuse steroids might spend up to $30,000 a year on them.

People who inject steroids—or illegal drugs such as heroin or cocaine—put themselves at an even greater

risk. Using hypodermic needles to inject drugs can increase the user's risk of contracting **hepatitis** (an inflammation of the liver). It can also increase the risk of being infected with **HIV** (human immunodeficiency virus). HIV is the virus responsible for **AIDS** (acquired immune deficiency syndrome), an often deadly disease for which there is currently no cure.

Hiding the Truth

Many athletes who take steroids also consume **masking agents**—substances that "mask" or hide traces of the drug so that it cannot be detected during drug tests. In addition, some steroids are **water-soluble**, meaning that an athlete who stops taking them within two weeks of a test will usually show no traces of the drug in the urine.

Cheating on drug tests has become so prevalent that officials must now watch athletes urinate to confirm that the urine samples they submit are actually their own. Even so, some athletes who abuse drugs have gone to incredible extremes to ensure that they do not fail urine tests while abusing steroids. In a few cases, a dishonest athlete has managed to put another person's drug-free urine into his own bladder by inserting a catheter (tube) into his urethra before the test.

Two Sides to Every Story: Steroids That Help

When used properly, steroids help alleviate the symptoms of some diseases and give many people great comfort and relief from pain. One of the biggest differ-

When prescribed by physicians and used properly, steroids can provide pain relief for diseases such as rheumatoid arthritis and lupus, and conditions like osteoporosis, which commonly affects elderly women.

ences between these drugs and those used by athletes to bulk up is that these substances are prescribed in small doses by medical doctors who are familiar with the drugs' possible side effects. These doctors tell patients what to expect so that they can watch for dangerous symptoms. Additionally, steroids taken for medicinal purposes are nearly always discontinued after being

taken for a short period of time, so that any dangerous side effects are minimized.

A different type of steroid, known as a **cortico-steroid**, is often prescribed by doctors to reduce inflammation and swelling. This type of drug is known as an **anti-inflammatory**. When a person sprains an ankle, for example, the area begins to swell, and the cells surrounding the ankle produce hormone-like substances called **prostaglandins** that stimulate nearby nerve cells, thereby increasing pain. Corticosteroids help reduce pain by reducing the inflammation that results after an injury. Corticosteroids have also been used to treat adults who have **rheumatoid arthritis**, a chronic disease that causes pain, stiffness, inflammation, swelling, and sometimes destruction of the joints. Recently, scientists also discovered that corticosteroids injected directly into the joints can safely and effectively help children with rheumatoid arthritis.

Steroids can alleviate the symptoms of some allergy sufferers and of people who are diagnosed with **lupus**, a disease that attacks the body's skin and connective tissues. Steroids have also been prescribed to treat diseases such as cancer, muscular dystrophy, and diabetes. They can improve appetite, aid healing, help elderly people absorb protein, and help slow the progression of **osteoporosis** (bone loss, often experienced by elderly women).

Do They or Don't They?

When people abuse most drugs, they can expect to look unhealthy. People who abuse cocaine or other dangerous stimulants, for example, may display difficulty concentrating and suffer from muscle pain, blurry vision, and tremors. Marijuana abusers sometimes have trouble remembering or learning things, and they have poor muscle coordination. Looking at these people, you would probably be able to tell that they were not in the best of health.

On the other hand, steroid users may appear deceptively big, strong, and healthy. Maybe this is why steroid abuse is considered less serious than the abuse of other drugs. But make no mistake: steroids are powerful drugs, and when used improperly they are illegal. When prescribed by doctors to treat serious medical problems like arthritis or lupus, they can improve a patient's health. But they also have potentially serious side effects, especially in young people.

Want to perform better, grow stronger, and have more energy? Try eating a healthy diet instead of turning to quick-fix solutions like steroids.

5

GETTING REAL: FIGHTING STEROID ABUSE

Have you ever sat on the beach or at a public swimming pool and watched the people who walk by? They come in every imaginable shape and size. When you really think about it, how many people have you ever seen who have what society considers the "perfect" body? Not many, to be sure.

Unfortunately, the physical ideals we have in our minds are hard to achieve in reality. Most men are not gigantic hunks of muscle, and most women are not thin with curves in all the "right" places. Instead of striving for unrealistic ideals, we should take pride in what we have and strive to maintain a fit body and a healthy mind. Yet one study conducted in 1995 shows that 5 to 10 percent of all adolescent boys have used steroids because they are not happy with their bodies.

As we discussed in Chapter 1, young people often

view athletes as role models. They may want to be like them, perform like them, and look like them. It is fun—and healthy—to admire role models, but it is also important to develop your own sense of purpose in life. This can be hard, but it is easier than forcing your body to become something it isn't meant to be through the abuse of steroids.

Some people believe that if only they were muscular enough or lean enough, everyone would admire them and their lives would be happy. But this fantasy is as unreal as *Alice's Adventures in Wonderland*. It takes courage and strength to accept yourself as you are, rather than trying to conform to an impossible ideal.

The next time you look in the mirror, look at your whole body. Try to find features that you like about yourself. Celebrate and enjoy your good points. Everybody has them! Over time, it will become easier to find what you like about yourself. You'll also learn that it's easier to like your body than to become obsessed about your real or imagined appearance.

Some Reasons Why People Use Drugs

We all know what it feels like to want to belong to a group. No one wants to feel disliked or left out. But what happens when someone in the group does something you don't agree with or don't want to do? Even if you don't want to use drugs like steroids, for example, everyone else on your sports team seems to be doing it. You don't want to go against the crowd by refusing. What do you do?

The feeling you experience when you're in a situation like this is called **peer pressure**. That is, a peer—a friend, a brother or sister, or someone else of your own age or generation—does or says something to make you feel like you have to act the same way to fit in.

Sometimes, peer pressure is easy to spot. A person might come right out and say something to make you feel bad. "Come on, don't be a baby," your friend might say, or "Everyone else is doing it." Other times, it's not so easy to see. Even if your friends don't say anything, you may still worry that they won't like you or will think less of you if you don't go along with them.

If you think about it, people who tell you that you can have the perfect body by using steroids are using the same kind of pressure you may feel from your friends or classmates. They are in the business of selling steroids to make money, not to make you feel or look better.

Knowledge Is Power

The more you understand about how a drug works and what it does to you, the better equipped you are to make an intelligent decision to turn it down. For example, most young adults know that steroids enhance muscle development and athletic performance. But how many kids understand the long-term health effects? If more people knew that taking steroids can stunt growth and damage the liver and heart, would 5 to 10 percent of adolescent boys continue taking them? Probably not.

Almost all drugs have side effects. Even cold remedies you buy at the drugstore can be harmful if they are

In 1998 baseball great Mark McGwire admitted that he uses androstenedione to build muscle and help heal injuries. Although the substance is a steroid, the National Baseball League does not prohibit its use. What do you think about steroid use among professional athletes? Do you feel pressure to use these drugs to compete in your favorite sport?

not used according to directions. Talk to your parents, a teacher, or another adult you trust for more information about drugs. Or track down the facts yourself. You can find information at your local library or on the Internet. Many schools and communities also offer drug awareness programs, seminars, books, and videotapes that will help you learn more. One advantage that today's kids have over previous generations is the great volume of information available to them from sources such as these.

Winning at All Costs

Everyone loves a winner. And successful athletes can earn a lot of money. In this atmosphere, it is easy to forget that winning isn't everything, even though it seems to be for some people. A 1995 poll of 198 Olympic-level athletes showed that more than half of those surveyed said they would take a drug that would assure them victory but would also kill them in five years. This is a frightening statistic!

Baseball pro Mark McGwire, who became a huge sports hero when he broke Roger Maris's single-season home-run record in 1998, has admitted that he uses a steroid called **androstenedione**, claiming that it increases the efficiency of his weight-room workouts and helps him heal from injuries. Even though this substance is legal in the United States—and is allowed in the major leagues—it has already been banned by the NFL and the International Olympic Committee, and

Did You Know?

Five to 10 percent of all adolescent boys use steroids, according to a study done for the *Clinical Journal of Sports Medicine* in 1995. Unfortunately, students who show a greater intent to use steroids also show a greater intent to abuse other drugs, such as alcohol and marijuana.

researchers are not sure how safe or effective it is. When young athletes see the adulation lavished on sports stars like McGwire, staying drug-free can be challenging.

From an early age, we are bombarded with unrealistic images. Boys may play with hyper-muscular action figures and girls with thin and voluptuous Barbie dolls. But there are also real-life role models who are paving the way toward healthier ideals for young people like you. Bodybuilding champs Arnold Schwarzenegger and

Did you know that regular exercise can help you feel less stressed? It also helps you tone your body and keeps your organs in good condition. Along with a good diet and regular sleep, exercise is the best thing youngsters can do to keep their bodies and minds healthy.

Lee Haney and Minnesota governor Jesse Ventura, who was formerly a professional wrestler, have spoken out against steroid use. Major magazines, ranging from *Newsweek* to *Sports Illustrated*, have published articles warning about the dangers of steroid abuse.

A Quick Fix or a Long Life?

We type in a keyword on the Internet and—voilà!— our computer screens brim with information. We sit in front of the TV and click the remote control until we find what we want to watch. Supersonic jets carry us across the world at speeds that were once thought unimaginable. Even when we want something to eat, we can pop food into a microwave and have a snack or dinner ready in minutes. It seems that we can get almost anything "right now."

But quicker is not always better, especially in the case of steroids. What seems like a fast way to look good and build muscle can cost you your health or even your life. Following a healthy diet and getting regular exercise and plenty of rest are far better ways to make your body strong. Not only are these practices safer and cheaper, but they are also much easier to achieve than maintaining a lifestyle that includes "cycling" on steroids. What's more, when you eat well and exercise regularly, you can become a role model for younger children.

Exercise Your Right to a Healthy Mind and Body

When you exercise regularly and eat well, your heart, lungs, and other organs stay healthy. Your skin and hair look better, you feel energetic, and you sleep more soundly. You may not realize it, but regular exercise also helps keep your mind in shape. It eliminates stress and makes you feel more alert and refreshed.

If you really want to build muscle or increase your athletic performance, look into a program of lifting weights or doing aerobic exercises. Under proper supervision, you will be able to tone and build muscle without using steroids.

A Healthy Diet: You'll Like It!

The U.S. Department of Agriculture released a set of dietary guidelines that Americans should follow if they want to stay healthy and reduce their risk of getting certain ailments and diseases. Here is a list of what you should try to eat every day:

Bread, cereal, rice, and pasta (carbohydrates):
6 to 11 servings

Vegetables:
3 to 5 servings

Fruits (fresh, frozen, canned, dried, or juices):
2 to 4 servings

Meat, poultry, fish, beans, eggs, and nuts (proteins):
2 to 3 servings

Milk, yogurt, and cheese (dairy products):
2 to 3 servings

Fats, oils, and sweets:
use sparingly

Becoming health-conscious can help you respect your body and avoid the things that harm it, such as steroids and other drugs. If you are exercising and eating healthfully, it seems a lot easier to say no to drugs.

Everyone knows the benefits of eating healthful foods. But young athletes who are still growing need to pay especially close attention to their diets, since they use much more energy than an average person. Teens aged 15 to 18 years old are continuing to grow and must refuel their bodies frequently. It is important to eat a wide variety of foods as well. Look at the chart on page 64 for a list of what you should try to eat every day.

In addition to eating foods from the groups listed, don't forget to drink plenty of water (six to eight glasses per day), which keeps the body hydrated and flushes out impurities. Remember that when you exercise a lot, you sweat more, and you can become dehydrated if you don't replace the fluid you lose.

How Can I Help Fight Steroid Abuse?

How can you tell if a friend or loved one has a problem with steroid abuse? Read the list below for some indications.

- Problems with physical dexterity (difficulty picking things up or handling items such as silverware)
- Cheating, breaking rules, or defying authorities
- Needing more discipline or instructions
- Vandalizing, fighting, or having frequent angry outbursts
- Changing regular habits and activities
- Being hyperactive or nervous
- Taking more physical risks
- Gaining a significant amount of weight or muscle mass

- Having extreme mood swings
- Being verbally abusive
- Being depressed over a long period of time or withdrawing from others
- Physical changes in males: baldness, development of breasts, shrinking testicles
- Physical changes in females: growth of facial hair, deepened voice, changes in menstrual cycle

Keep in mind that some of these signs, such as mood changes, problems getting along with others, and depression, might indicate other problems. They may also be symptoms of an illness you may not know about. If someone you know seems to have a drug problem, you may want to talk to him or her to find out for sure. If you do, you may want to follow these suggestions:

- Plan ahead what you want to say and how to say it.
- Pick a quiet and private time to talk.
- Don't try to talk about the problem when the person is angry or upset.
- Use a calm voice, and don't get into an argument.
- Let your friend or relative know that you care. Ask whether you can do anything to help, such as finding a counseling or drug abuse treatment center, and offer to go along.
- Don't expect the person to like what you're saying. But stick with it—the more people express concern, the better the chances of your friend or loved one getting help.

Remember that it's not your job to get others to stop using drugs. You can offer help, but only they can decide whether to quit. Be sure that you also talk to an adult whom you trust or who is trained to recognize drug abuse. A doctor, nurse, religious leader, counselor, scout leader, coach, or parent can give you advice about what to do next.

Help Yourself!

If you have already tried steroids, you have probably discovered that they *can* make you feel and look better for a short time. But in the long run, steroids won't solve your troubles or improve your life. In fact, now that you know the facts about steroids, you have probably realized that using them will only make your problems worse. Often, drug use also creates new problems.

Don't forget that your physical appearance is only one of the many ways you can express yourself. Our looks are only a small component of who we are. An individual is just that—different from everyone else. We all want to fit in, but we also need to learn how to celebrate our differences in a healthy manner. There's probably someone out there who longs to be just like you— just the way you are right now.

addiction—physical dependence; a state in which a drug user's body has become dependent on the drug to function normally. An addicted user continues to take drugs, despite negative consequences. Obtaining and using the drug take over the person's life.

adrenal glands—a pair of endocrine organs near the kidney that produce androgenic hormones.

AIDS—acquired immune deficiency syndrome; a defect of the immune system caused by the human immunodeficiency virus (HIV). AIDS is spread by the exchange of blood and by sexual contact; intravenous drug users have an increased risk of contracting HIV and developing AIDS.

anabolic—mimicking the muscle-building effects of the male sex hormone testosterone. Anabolic (or "building") steroids are sometimes abused by athletes to build muscle temporarily while minimizing the masculinizing effects of testosterone.

androgen—a male sex hormone, such as testosterone, that is responsible for the development of masculine characteristics, such as the growth of body hair and deepening of the voice.

androgenic—mimicking the masculinizing effects of the male sex hormone testosterone. Along with anabolic steroids, androgenic (or "masculinizing") steroids are sometimes abused by athletes to build muscle temporarily.

androstenedione—an anabolic steroid used to build muscle.

anti-inflammatory—a substance that reduces inflammation or swelling.

artery—a vessel that carries blood from the heart to the rest of the body.

atherosclerosis—a disease characterized by deposits of fatty substances in the arteries that block the flow of blood from the heart to the rest of the body.

bile—a yellow or greenish fluid produced by the liver to aid in breaking down and absorbing fats.

black market—illegal trade in goods or commodities that violates official regulations. Some anabolic steroids are bought and sold on the black market.

clenbuterol—a so-called steroid alternative that, like steroids, is used to build muscle.

corticosteroid—a type of prescription steroid used to reduce swelling or inflammation. Since corticosteroids do not build muscles the way anabolic steroids do, people don't abuse them in the same way.

cycling—a pattern of taking multiple anabolic steroids over a specified period of time, then stopping for a time and starting again.

doping—taking performance-enhancing drugs or other non-food substances to improve athletic performance.

edema—an abnormally high accumulation of fluid in the body.

endocrine system—a group of glands, including the adrenal glands, the pancreas, the testes (in males), and the ovaries (in females), that secrete hormones into the blood to be carried to specific organs.

ergogenic drug—a substance, such as an anabolic steroid, that is taken for the purpose of building muscle or improving athletic performance. Ergogenic drugs are also known as performance-enhancing drugs.

erythropoietin (EPO)—a synthetic anabolic steroid that stimulates production of oxygen-rich blood cells. EPO is used to treat kidney disease, anemia, and other disorders, but it is also abused by some athletes who want to increase their stamina or endurance levels.

estrogen—a female sex hormone that stimulates the development of sex characteristics.

gallstone—a small, hard deposit of minerals that can form in the gallbladder or in the bile ducts.

gamma hydroxybutyrate (GHB)—also nicknamed "grievous bodily harm"; an "alternative" steroid that is abused by some athletes to build muscle. GHB is also abused by some people as a social drug to produce mild euphoria and relaxation.

gland—an organ in the body that makes a specific substance that the body uses or gives off. For example, the thyroid gland regulates body metabolism; the ovaries (in females) and testes (in males) influence sex characteristics.

hepatitis—a disease or condition marked by inflammation of the liver.

HIV—human immunodeficiency virus; the virus that causes AIDS.

hormone—a substance produced by a gland in the endocrine system and carried by the blood to body organs and tissue. Hormones regulate some body functions and control growth.

hypertension—high blood pressure.

hypothalamus—the area of the brain that is responsible for controlling appetite, blood pressure, moods, and production of testosterone.

limbic system—the area of the brain that is responsible for learning and memory.

lupus—also known as lupus erythematosus; a disorder characterized by skin inflammation.

lymph—a clear liquid that carries nourishment to bodily tissues and waste to the bloodstream.

masking agent—a substance that hides traces of an illegal drug in the body so that the drug cannot be detected in a drug test.

nandrolone—an anabolic steroid.

osteoporosis—a condition characterized by a decrease in bone mass and enlargement of bone spaces, so that the bones become more fragile and porous. Osteoporosis commonly affects older women.

ovaries—a part of a female human or animal in which egg cells and female sex hormones are produced.

pathologist—a scientist who specializes in the study of diseases in tissues and body fluids.

peer pressure—words or actions by a friend, a sibling, or someone else of your own age group that make you feel as though you have to act like them to fit in with the group.

performance-enhancing drug—a substance, such as an anabolic steroid, that is taken for the purpose of building muscle or improving athletic performance. Performance-enhancing drugs are also known as ergogenic drugs.

pharmaceutical—relating to a person who specializes in preparing medicines or drugs, or relating to the place where the drugs are manufactured or sold.

physical dependence—a state in which a drug user's body chemistry has adapted to require regular doses of the drug to function normally. Stopping the drug causes withdrawal.

progesterone—a female sex hormone that prepares the body for implantation of an egg.

prostaglandin—a substance produced by the body that performs hormone-like functions, such as regulating blood pressure or contracting muscles.

psychological dependence—the state of addiction in which certain brain changes create strong cravings to use a drug, even if the user has no withdrawal symptoms or physical urge to do so.

puberty—the physical onset of adulthood.

rheumatoid arthritis—a chronic disease characterized by stiffness, inflammation, swelling, and sometimes destruction of joints.

'roid rage—increased aggression, hostility, or destructive behavior caused by anabolic steroid abuse.

secretion—a substance, such as a hormone, that is produced by a bodily organ.

side effect—a secondary and usually bad effect, as with a drug.

stacking—using a combination of anabolic steroids and other drugs to promote optimal muscle growth.

testes—the male reproductive gland that produces sperm.

testosterone—a hormone that is responsible for male sex characteristics. Testosterone is produced mainly by the testes (in males), but females also produce a very small amount.

toxicology—the study of the nature, effects, and detection of poisons.

urine test—chemical analysis of a sample of urine for the purpose of detecting certain diseases, drugs, or substances in the body.

water-soluble—able to be dissolved in water.

withdrawal—a process that occurs when a person who is physically dependent on a drug stops taking the drug.

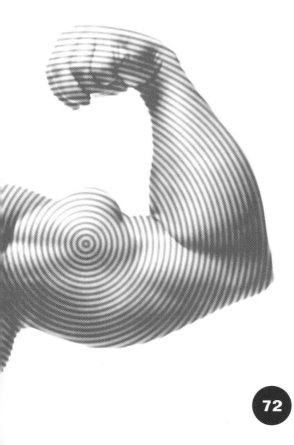

BIBLIOGRAPHY

Abt, Samuel. "Cyclists Stage Protest as Drug Investigation Widens." *New York Times*, 25 July 1998.

Bamberger, Michael, and Don Yaeger. "Over the Edge." *Sports Illustrated*, 14 April 1997.

Buck, Ray. "Steroids Build NFL Players Up—and Take Them Down, Too." *CBS Sportsline* (Internet), July 23, 1998.

Fields, Richard. *Drugs in Perspective: A Personalized Look at Substance Use and Abuse.* Boston, MA: McGraw-Hill, 1998.

Finn, Robin. "Teen-Ager's Steroid Case Reveals Tennis's Hidden Threat." *New York Times*, 19 August 1998.

Herbert, Bob. "In America: A Hero and His Shadow." *New York Times*, 27 August 1998.

Longenecker, Gesina L. *How Drugs Work: Drug Abuse and the Human Body.* Emeryville, CA: Ziff-Davis Press, 1994.

National Clearinghouse for Alcohol and Drug Information (NCADI). "Tips for Teens About Steroids." Rockville, MD: NCADI, 1999.

National Institute on Drug Abuse (NIDA). "Anabolic Steroids: A Threat to Mind and Body." NIDA Publication No. 97-3721. Rockville, MD: NIDA, 1996.

____. *Mind Over Matter: The Brain's Response to Steroids.* NIDA Publication No. 97-3860. Rockville, MD: NIDA/National Institutes of Health, 1997.

Peck, Rodney G. *Drugs and Sports.* New York: Rosen Publishing Group, 1998.

Yesalis, Charles E., ed. *Anabolic Steroids in Sport and Exercise.* Champaign, IL: Human Kinetics Publishers, 1993.

FIND OUT MORE ABOUT STEROIDS, SPORTS MEDICINE, AND DRUG ABUSE

The following list includes agencies, organizations, and websites that provide information about steroids, sports medicine, and drug abuse. You can also find out where to go for help with a drug problem.

Many national organizations have local chapters listed in your phone directory. Look under "Drug Abuse and Addiction" to find resources in your area.

Agencies and Organizations in the United States

**American Academy
of Sports Physicians**
17113 Gledhill Street
Northridge, CA 91325
818-886-7891

**American College
of Sports Medicine**
P.O. Box 1440
Indianapolis, IN 46206
317-637-9200

**American Council
for Drug Education**
164 West 74th Street
New York, NY 10023
212-758-8060 or 800-488-DRUG (3784)
http://www.acde.org/
wlittlefield@phoenixhouse.org

**American Orthopedic Society
for Sports Medicine**
2250 East Devon Avenue
Suite 115
Des Plaines, IL 60018
708-803-8700

**American Osteopathic
Academy of Sports Medicine**
7611 Elmwood Avenue
Suite 201
Middleton, WI 53562
608-831-4400

**Center for Substance
Abuse Treatment**
Information and Treatment Referral Hotline
11426-28 Rockville Pike, Suite 410
Rockville, MD 20852
800-622-HELP (4357)

Joint Commission on Sports Medicine and Science
Oklahoma State University
Student Health Center
Stillwater, OK 74078
405-744-7031

National Clearinghouse for Alcohol and Drug Information (NCADI)
P.O. Box 2345
Rockville, MD 20847-2345
800-729-6686

National Council on Alcoholism and Drug Dependence, Inc. (NCADD)
12 West 21st St., 7th Floor
New York, NY 10017
212-206-6770 or 800-NCA-CALL (622-2255)
http://www.ncadd.org/

Office of National Drug Control Policy
750 17th Street, N.W., Eighth Floor
Washington, DC 20503
http://www.whitehousedrugpolicy.gov/
ondcp@ncjrs.org
888-395-NDCP (6327)

Parents Resource Institute for Drug Education (PRIDE)
3610 Dekalb Technology Parkway, Ste 105
Atlanta, GA 30340
770-458-9900
http://www.prideusa.org/

Shalom, Inc.
311 South Juniper Street
Room 900
Philadelphia, PA 19107
215-546-3470

Agencies and Organizations in Canada

Addictions Foundation of Manitoba
1031 Portage Avenue
Winnipeg, Manitoba R3G 0R8
204-944-6277
http://www.mbnet.mb.ca/crm/health/afm.html

Addiction Research Foundation (ARF)
33 Russell Street
Toronto, Ontario M5S 2S1
416-595-6100
800-463-6273 in Ontario

Alberta Alcohol and Drug Abuse Commission
10909 Jasper Avenue, 6th Floor
Edmonton, Alberta T5J 3M9
http://www.gov.ab.ca/aadac/

British Columbia Prevention Resource Centre
96 East Broadway, Suite 211
Vancouver, British Columbia V5T 1V6
604-874-8452
800-663-1880 (BC only)

**Canadian Centre
on Substance Abuse**

75 Albert Street, Suite 300

Ottawa, Ontario K1P 5E7

613-235-4048

http://www.ccsa.ca/

**Ontario Healthy
Communities Central Office**

180 Dundas Street West, Suite 1900

Toronto, Ontario M5G 1Z8

416-408-4841

http://www.opc.on.ca/ohcc/

**Saskatchewan Health
Resource Centre**

Saskatchewan Health, T.C. Douglas Building

3475 Albert Street

Regina, Saskatchewan S4S 6X6

306-787-3090

Websites

**D.A.R.E. (Drug Abuse
Resistance Education)
for Kids**

http://www.dare-america.com/index2.htm

Drug Strategy Institute

http://www2.druginfo.org/orgs/dsi

**FDA (Food and Drug
Administration) Kids
Home Page**

http://www.fda.gov/oc/opacom/kids/

Kids Food Cyber Club

http://www.kidsfood.org

**National Institute
on Drug Abuse (NIDA)**

http://www.nida.nih.gov/

**Partnership for a
Drug-Free America**

http://www.drugfreeamerica.org/

Despite what you may have heard, selling illegal drugs will not make you rich. In 1998, two professors, Steven Levitt from the University of Chicago and Sudhir Venkatesh from Harvard University, released a study of how drug gangs make and distribute money. To get accurate information, Venkatesh actually lived with a drug gang in a midwestern city.

You may be surprised to find out that the average street dealer makes just about $3 an hour. You'd make more money working at McDonald's! Still think drug-dealing is a cool way to make money? What other after-school jobs carry the risk of going to prison or dying in the street from a gunshot wound?

Drug-dealing is illegal, and it kills people. If you're thinking of selling drugs or you know someone who is, ask yourself this question: is $3 an hour worth dying for or being imprisoned?

WHAT A DRUG GANG MAKES IN A MONTH*

	During a Gang War	No Gang War
INCOME (money coming in)	$ 44,500	$ 58,900
Other income (including dues and blackmail money)	10,000	18,000
TOTAL INCOME	**$ 54,500**	**$ 76,900**
EXPENSES (money paid out)		
Cost of drugs sold	$ 11,300	$ 12,800
Wages for officers and street pushers	25,600	37,600
Weapons	3,000	1,600
Tributes (fees) paid to central gang	5,800	5,900
Funeral and other expenses	10,300	4,200
TOTAL EXPENSES	**$ 56,000**	**$ 62,100**
TOTAL INCOME	$ 54,000	$ 76,900
MINUS TOTAL EXPENSES	- 56,000	- 62,100
TOTAL AMOUNT OF PROFIT IN ONE MONTH	**- 1,500**	**14,800**

* adapted from "Greedy Bosses," *Forbes*, August 24, 1998, p. 53. Source: Levitt and Venkatesh.

Addiction, 44-47
Adrenal glands, 42, 43
Aggression, 23, 28, 41-42, 65, 66
AIDS (acquired immune deficiency syndrome), 52
Alzado, Lyle, 14-15, 16
Anabolic Steroids Act of 1990, 37
Androgen, 34, 42
Androstenedione, 61
Anti-Drug Abuse Act of 1988, 37

Binus, Dieter, 19
Brain, the, 14, 15, 41-42, 44
Brain lymphoma, 15

Cancer, 14-15, 35, 49, 54
Clenbuterol, 20, 22
Clinical Journal of Sports Medicine, 61
Corticosteroids, 54
Courson, Steve, 38
Cycling, 50-51

Dietary guidelines, 64-65
Donovan, Pat, 36
Doping, 33
Drug awareness programs, 60
Drug tests, 17, 19-20, 36-37, 52

Endocrine system, 41, 42
Ergogenic drugs, 16
Estrogen, 43

Gamma hydroxybutyrate (GHB), 20-22

Halloway (racehorse), 35
Haney, Lee, 62
Harris, Ronald, 27

Heart disorders, 49-50, 59
Henderson, Thomas "Hollywood," 16
HIV (human immunodeficiency virus), 52
Hormones, 15, 34, 42
Human growth hormones, 15
Hypothalamus, the, 42, 44

Internet, the, 30-31, 60, 62

Johnson, Ben, 17
Jones, Alan, 20

Kerr, Robert, 18
Kidneys, 23, 36
Klecko, Joe, 36

Limbic system, 41
Liver, 47-49, 52, 59

McGwire, Mark, 61
Maracescu, Natalia, 30
Masking agents, 52

Nor-Andro 19, 20

Pacifico, Larry, 50
Peer pressure, 59
Performance-enhancing drugs, 16, 17, 30
Petrova, Totka, 30
Professional sports, steroid use in
   baseball, 61
   cycling, 36
   football, 14-16, 36, 38, 61
   the Olympics, 17, 30, 35-37, 61
   tennis, 20
   weightlifting, 22-23, 50, 61-62

Progesterone, 43
Prostaglandins, 54

Reeves, Samantha, 19
Rheumatoid arthritis, 54
'Roid rage. *See* Aggression

Sandlin, Richard L., 22-23
Schwarzenegger, Arnold, 61
Smerlas, Fred, 36

Stacking, 50-51

Testes, 42, 43, 44
Testicular atrophy, 23
Testosterone, 34, 35, 42, 43-44, 47

Ventura, Jesse, 62

Waddell, Tom, 35-36
Withdrawal, 46-47

PICTURE CREDITS

DYNISE BALCAVAGE is a writer and graphic designer who lives in Philadelphia. She is the author of *Ludwig van Beethoven* (Chelsea House, 1997). Balcavage also writes for several magazines including *The Georgia Review*, *Desktop Publishers Journal*, and *Spin-Off*.

BARRY R. McCAFFREY is director of the Office of National Drug Control Policy (ONDCP) at the White House and a member of President Bill Clinton's cabinet. Before taking this job, General McCaffrey was an officer in the U.S. Army. He led the famous "left hook" maneuver of Operation Desert Storm that helped the United States win the Persian Gulf War.

STEVEN L. JAFFE, M.D., received his psychiatry training at Harvard University and the Massachusetts Mental Health Center and his child psychiatry training at Emory University. He has been editor of the *Newsletter of the American Academy of Child and Adolescent Psychiatry* and chairman of the Continuing Education Committee of the Georgia Psychiatric Physicians' Association. Dr. Jaffe is professor of child and adolescent psychiatry at Emory University. He is also clinical professor of psychiatry at Morehouse School of Medicine, and the director of Adolescent Substance Abuse Programs at Charter Peachford Hospital in Atlanta, Georgia.